"A discourse of Virginia."

Edward Maria Wingfield, Charles Deane

Nabu Public Domain Reprints:

You are holding a reproduction of an original work published before 1923 that is in the public domain in the United States of America, and possibly other countries. You may freely copy and distribute this work as no entity (individual or corporate) has a copyright on the body of the work. This book may contain prior copyright references, and library stamps (as most of these works were scanned from library copies). These have been scanned and retained as part of the historical artifact.

This book may have occasional imperfections such as missing or blurred pages, poor pictures, errant marks, etc. that were either part of the original artifact, or were introduced by the scanning process. We believe this work is culturally important, and despite the imperfections, have elected to bring it back into print as part of our continuing commitment to the preservation of printed works worldwide. We appreciate your understanding of the imperfections in the preservation process, and hope you enjoy this valuable book.

Jared Sparks, LL.D.

*with the respects of
the Editor*

"A DISCOURSE OF VIRGINIA."

BY

EDWARD MARIA WINGFIELD,

THE FIRST PRESIDENT OF THE COLONY

Now first printed from the Original Manuscript in the Lambeth Library

---

𝔈𝔡𝔦𝔱𝔢𝔡, 𝔴𝔦𝔱𝔥 𝔑𝔬𝔱𝔢𝔰 𝔞𝔫𝔡 𝔞𝔫 𝔍𝔫𝔱𝔯𝔬𝔡𝔲𝔠𝔱𝔦𝔬𝔫,

BY CHARLES DEANE,

MEMBER OF THE AMERICAN ANTIQUARIAN SOCIETY, AND OF THE MASSACHUSETTS
HISTORICAL SOCIETY

BOSTON.
PRIVATELY PRINTED
1860.

FROM AMERICAN ANTIQUARIAN SOCIETY'S TRANSACTIONS, VOL. IV.

One Hundred Copies privately Printed.

BOSTON: PRINTED BY JOHN WILSON AND SON.

WINGFIELD'S DISCOURSE OF VIRGINIA.

INTRODUCTION.

About three years since, my attention was first directed to this narrative of Wingfield in the Lambeth Library, by the reference made to it in the first volume of the Rev. James S. M. Anderson's "History of the Church of England in the Colonies," &c., first published in London in 1845. In lamenting the lack of definite information concerning the Rev. Robert Hunt, the first minister in the Colony, the author says, " I am thankful, however, to have found in the Lambeth Library a manuscript which throws some light, however faint, upon this latter point. It is marked in the catalogue as 'anonymous'; and the description is so far correct, that its author's name is not formally inscribed upon it. The dedication is not signed at all, but, perceiving that it was a journal of the earliest proceedings of the Colony, I felt persuaded that it would well repay perusal. Nor was I disappointed; for I found it written by a person of no less importance than Edward Maria Wingfield, — one of those to whom the patent was granted, and who, upon the arrival of the colonists in Virginia, was elected their first President. It contains a minute account of the transactions which chiefly concerned himself, from the time of their first landing in Virginia to his return to England, after he had been deposed from his office. . . . I am not aware that its contents have in any shape been placed before the public" (vol. i. p 167, second edition, London, 1856) The author, in the preface, expresses his obligation to the Rev. S. R Maitland, Librarian at Lambeth, for the help which he afforded in deciphering the manuscript

The application for a copy of this manuscript, which I at once formed the purpose of making, was delayed until within a few months; when one was promptly procured for me through my friend, Mr. H. G. Somerby, of London, who, in a note respecting the original, thus writes: "The journal fills about twenty pages of foolscap paper, and is closely written Mr. Anderson is wrong in stating that it is marked 'anonymous' in the catalogue. That word refers to another manuscript.

Mr. Wingfield's name is indorsed on the back of the journal." In a note accompanying the copy, he says, "I have carefully compared the copy with the original, and corrected several mistakes made by the copyist, so that you can rely upon the document I send you, *verbatim et literatim*" The indorsement upon the journal, which is in vol 250 of MSS pp. 383 *et seq*, is, "A Discourse of Virginia. Auct. Ed. Ma. Wingfield."

Since the time of Purchas, who probably had seen this narrative (see vol. iv. p. 1706), it appears to have escaped the notice of historical students till the attention of Mr Anderson was attracted to it As will be seen, the "Discourse" is written in part, if not chiefly, in defence of the author's course while President of the Colony, and in reply to the charges preferred against him; and was probably drawn up soon after his return to England in May, 1608.

The only original Histories of the Colony at Jamestown, hitherto published, covering the period embraced by this manuscript, are, — First, the one by Capt John Smith, giving a history of the settlement from the arrival of the colonists in April, 1607, to the sailing of Capt Nelson in the "Phœnix," June 2, 1608 This may have been sent over by that vessel, as it was printed the same year, in a small quarto of thirty-six pages, in black letter, with the following title: —

"A True Relation of such occurrences and accidents of noate as hapned in Virginia since the first planting of that Collony, which is now resident in the south part thereof, till the last returne from thence. Written by Captaine Smith, coronell of the said Collony, to a worshipfull friend of his in England. London, . . . 1608."

It may be mentioned, that the title first issued with this tract, by a mistake of the printer, bore the name of Thomas Watson as the author. With the corrected title was added an explanatory preface. This is the first tract published relating to the Colony at Jamestown

Second, the description of Virginia by Capt. Smith, entitled —

"A Map of Virginia. With a Description of the Countrey, the Commodities, People, Government, and Religion. Written by Captaine Smith, sometimes Governour of the Countrey. Whereunto is annexed the Proceedings of those Colonies, since their first Departure from England, with the discourses, Orations, and relations of the Salvages, and the accidents that befell them in all their Journeys and discoveries. Taken faithfvlly as they were written out of the writings of Doctor Rvssell, Tho. Stvdley, Anas Todkill, Ieffra Abot, Richard Wiffin, Will. Phettiplace, Nathaniel Powell, Richard Pots, . . At Oxford, . . . 1612."

The first part of this tract, purporting to be written by Smith, is, as its title indicates, a topographical description of the country. It was prefaced by his map of Virginia, first published here. In a letter addressed to the Treasurer and Council of the Virginia Company in England, written from Virginia after the arrival of Newport, in September, 1608, and probably sent home by him near the close of the year, Smith says, "I have sent you this map of the bay and rivers, with an annexed relation of the countries, and nations that inhabit them, as you may see at large" ("Generall Historie," pp 71, 72). The appendix to this book, written chiefly by the companions of Smith, contains a history of the Colony, more or less minute, from its commencement to the time when Capt. Smith left the country in the latter part of the year 1609; and some incidents even of a later date are added

Third, Percy's narrative, in Purchas, vol iv pp. 1685-1690, entitled —

"Observations gathered out of a Discourse of the Plantations of the Southern Colonie in Virginia by the English, 1606 Written by that Honorable Gentleman, Master George Percy."

The writer was a brother of the Earl of Northumberland. He was one of the first colonists, and subsequently a temporary governor of the plantation. To what period this narrative was brought down by the writer, we have no means of knowing; as Purchas has unfortunately preserved only an abridgment of it, in six of his folio pages, breaking off at September, 1607. This contains a minute and interesting account of the incidents of the first voyage, which are but briefly touched upon by the other narrators, and some details of the Colony are given, to be met with nowhere else

The above may be said to embrace all the original Histories of the Colony that have been published, covering the period named, one of them extending over a longer period A few additional incidents, here and there, may be gathered from other sources, particularly from some of Smith's later publications. His "Generall Historie," first published in 1624, — which is chiefly a compilation of other works, — embraces the tract of 1612, and some incidents from the earlier one; and occasionally introduces matter not to be found in either. The work of Strachey, — first published by the Hakluyt Society in 1849, — so far as it relates to Southern Virginia, is mainly a description of the natural history of the country, rather than an account of the English Colony there resident. He did not arrive in Virginia till 1610. A considerable portion of Smith's tract of 1612 has been adopted by him, and interwoven into his own narrative, without acknowledgment. Stith's volume I do not embrace in this category of original narratives for the early period covered by Wingfield's manuscript; though he is referred to for the letters-patent and orders and instructions from his Majesty, under which the Colony was first settled. The history of the Colony, therefore, for the period which chiefly interests us here, — and, indeed, for a year or two beyond, — is mainly derived from the writings of Smith and his companions. Through these, Wingfield, the first President, has been handed down in no favorable light. Several charges have been made against him, hitherto unanswered. His spirited narrative and defence, now for the first time published, will be read with interest.

The letters-patent under which the settlement at Jamestown was made were granted April 10, 1606. Besides these, the King issued divers instructions and orders, under his sign-manual and the privy seal, dated Nov. 20, 1606. The charter established a Treasurer and Council, to be resident in England, to consist of thirteen persons; and the same number was to constitute a Council resident in the Colony. The transportation of the persons designed for the Colony was committed to Capt. Christopher Newport, who had the sole charge and command of the same till they should land on the coast of Virginia. Three ships, whose names are preserved by Purchas, transported the company, — the "Susan Constant," admiral, of one hundred tons, commanded by Capt. Newport; the "God-speed," vice-admiral, of forty tons, commanded by Capt. Bartholomew Gosnold, the "Discovery," rear-admiral (the pinnace), of twenty tons, commanded by Capt. John Ratcliffe. They set sail on the 19th of December, 1606; but, by unprosperous winds, were kept in sight of England six weeks. They "watered at the Canaries;" passed several weeks among some of the West-India Islands, where they "refreshed themselves;" and did not reach the coast of Virginia till the 26th of April, 1607. On the night of their arrival, the box containing their orders for government was opened, and the papers, announcing who were appointed of the Council, were read. Until the 13th of May, the colonists were seeking a place for a settlement, about which all were not agreed Finally "they resolved on a peninsula, on the north of the River Powhatan, about forty miles from the mouth." There the government was inaugurated; the Council was sworn, and Wingfield, one of that body, was chosen President.

Before the colonists arrived on the coast, a modification of his Majesty's Council in England for Virginia had taken place, and subsequently other charters were granted.

Boston, Dec. 1, 1859.

"A DISCOURSE OF VIRGINIA."

Right Worp^{ull} and more worthy :[1]—

My due respect to yourselves, my allegiance (if I may so terme it) to the Virginean action, my good heed to my poore reputacõn, thrust a penne into my handes; so iealous am I to bee missing to any of them If it wandereth in extravagantes, yet shall they not bee idle to those physitions whose loves have undertaken the saftie and advancement of Virginia.

It is no small comfort that I speake before such gravitie, whose iudgement no forrunner can forestall with any opprobrious vntruths, whose wisedomes can easily disroabe malice out of her painted garments from the ever reverenced truth.

I did so faithfully betroth my best endeavours to this noble enterprize, as my carriage might endure no suspition. I never turned my face from daunger, or hidd my handes from labour; so watchfull a sentinel stood myself to myself. I know wel, a troope of errors continually beseege men's actions; some of them ceased on by malice, some by ignorance. I doo not hoodwinck my carriage in my self love, but freely and humblie submit it to your grave censures.

---

[1] Addressed, doubtless, to his Majesty's Council, in England, for Virginia

I do freely and truely anatomize the governement and governours, that your experience may applie medicines accordinglie; and vpon the truth of this iournal do pledge my faith and life, and so do rest

Yours to command in all service.[2]

Here followeth what happened in James Towne, in Virginia, after Captayne Newport's departure for Englaund

Captayne Newport,[3] haueing allwayes his eyes and eares open to the proceedings of the Collonye, 3 or 4 dayes before his departure asked the President how he thought himself settled in the gouernment: whose answere was, that no disturbance could indaunger him or the Collonye, but it must be wrought eyther by Captayne Gosnold or Mr Archer;[4] for the one was strong wth freinds and followers, and could if he would; and the other was troubled wth an ambitious spirit, and would if he could

---

[2] The above comprises the first page in the manuscript Mr Somerby writes that it "is in a different hand from the rest, and it wants the signature, as does the body of the manuscript."

[3] Capt Newport "was esteemed a marinei of ability and experience on the American coasts· for he had, fourteen years before (anno 1592), with much reputation and honor, conducted an expedition against the Spaniards in the West Indies, where, with three ships and a small bark, he took several prizes, plundered and burnt some towns, and got a considerable booty." — *Stith*, p 42 He was a member of the first Colonial Council — *Ibid*, p. 45.

[4] The names of Bartholomew Gosnold and Gabriel Archer are too well known to students of New-England history to need further mention here. One of the writers in the Appendix to Smith's Virginia (Oxford, 1612) says that the former was the "first mover" of the plantation of Virginia

The Captayne gave them both knowledge of this, the President's opinion; and moued them, with many intreaties, to be myndefull of their dutyes to His Matie and the Collonye.

June, 1607. — The 22th,[5] Captayne Newport retorned for England; for whose good passadge and safe retorne wee made many prayers to our Almighty God.

June the 25th, an Indian came to us from the great Poughwaton wth the word of peace; that he desired greatly our freindshipp, that the wyrounnces,[6] Pasyaheigh and Tapahanagh,[7] should be our freindes; that wee should sowe and reape in peace, or els he would make warrs vpon them wth vs. This message fell out true; for both those wyroaunces haue ever since remayned in peace and trade with vs. Wee

---

[5] In the tract last named, the date given for Newport's return is June 15, and some later writers have adopted that. But the date in the text is confirmed by Smith, in his first tract on Virginia, entitled "True Relation," &c., 1608 (a black-letter volume, not paged), by Percy in Purchas, vol. iv p. 1689, and by the writer of the journal of Newport's "Discoveries in Virginia," in Archæologia Americana, vol iv p 58 Newport left 104 colonists at Jamestown. — *Percy,* as above In the Appendix to Smith's "Virginia," p 8, the number of the "first planters" is stated to be 105, but in the list of names, so far as there given, that of Anthony Gosnold is inserted twice

[6] "His [Powhatan's] inferior kings, whom they call Werowances, are tied to rule by customs, and have power of life and death, as their command in that nature. But this word Werowance, which we call and conster for a king, is a common word whereby they call all commanders, for they have but few words in their language, and but few occasions to use any officers more than one commander." — *Smith's Virginia,* p 36

[7] The residence of Pasyaheigh, or, as the name is usually written, Paspahegh, may have been at the spot bearing that name, which is indicated on Smith's map of Virginia as a few miles above Jamestown, on the James River The name "Paspahegh" appears to have been applied by the Indians to the territory which embraced Jamestown — See *Hamor's True Discovrie,* &c. (London, 1615), p 88 For the residence of Tapahanah, see note 6, page 16

rewarded the messinger wth many tryfles wch were great wonders to him.

This Powatan[8] dwelleth 10 myles from vs, upon the River Pamaonche, wch lyeth North from vs. The Powatan in the former iornall[9] menc̃oned (a dwellar by Captn. Newport's faults[1]) ys a wyroaunce, and vnder this Great Powaton, wch before wee knew not.

July.—Th 3 of July, 7 or 8 Indians presented the President a dear from Pamaonke,[2] a wyrouance, desiring our friendshipp. They enquired after our shipping; wch the President said was gon to Croutoon.[3] They fear much our shipps, and therefore he would not haue them think it farr from us. Their wyrounce had a hatchet sent him. They wear well contented wth trifles. A little after this came a

---

[8] He was the "chief ruler," or "emperor," of that part of the country. His principal residence, at this time, was at a place called Werowocomoco, "upon the north side of York River."—*Stith*, p 53. "Some fourteen miles from Jamestown," says Smith, in his "Virginia," p 34, where the reader will find a particular description of this chief, and a more full one by Strachey, in his "Historie of Travaile in Virginia Britannia," pp 48–50.

[9] Perhaps the journal of Newport's Discoveries, Archæol Amer, vol iv p. 40 It is not improbable that the Powhatan visited by Newport was a son of the emperor — See *Strachey*, p 56. Smith was with Newport at this time, and it is quite certain, from all the narratives, that the former first saw the Emperor Powhatan at Werowocomoco, when brought before him as a prisoner, in December or January following — See *Smith's Virginia*, Appendix, p 14, *True Relation*.

[1] *Sic.*

[2] Probably Opechancanough, King of Pamaunkey, seated on the river of that name, the main part of which is now called York River — See *Smith's Virginia*, Appendix, pp 66, 67, *True Relation*, *Stith*, p 53, *Archæol Amer*, vol iv pp 52, 53

[3] Croaton was an Indian town on the south part of Cape Lookout, the place to which, it was supposed, the Colony, or the remnant of the Colony, left by Gov White at Roanoke in 1587, had gone, and concerning whom all subsequent search had proved fruitless

dear to the President from the Great Powatan He and his messingers were pleased wth the like trifles. The President likewise bought diuers tymes dear of the Indyans; beavers, and other flesh; wch he alwayes caused to be equally deuided among the Collonye.

About this tyme, diuers of our men fell sick. We myssed aboue fforty before September did see us,[4] amongst whom was the worthy and religious gent. Captn. Bartholomew Gosnold,[5] vpon whose liefs stood a great part of the good succes and fortune of our gouernment and Collony In his sicknes tyme, the President did easily foretel his owne deposing from his comaund; so much differed the President and the other Councellors in mannaging the government of the Collonye.

July.— The 7th of July, Tapahanah, a wyroaunce, dweller on Salisbery[6] side, hayled us with the word of peace. The President, wth a shallopp well manned, went to him. He found him sytting on the ground crossed legged, as is theire custom, w^h one attending on him, wch did often saie, "This is the wyroance Tapahanah;" wch he did likewise confirme wth stroaking his brest He was well enough knowne; for the Presi-

---

[4] "About the 10th of September, there was about forty-six of our men dead "— *True Relation* "From May to September, those that escaped lived upon sturgeon and sea-crabs fifty in this time we buried "— *Studley*, in Smith's Virginia, p 10

[5] "The two and twentieth day of August, there died Capt Bartholomew Gosnold, one of our Council He was honorably buried, having all the ordnance in the fort shot off, with many volleys of small shot." — *Percy*, in Purchas, vol iv. p 1690

[6] "Coracohanauke — which we commonly (though corruptly) call Tapahanock, and is the same which Capt. Smith, in his map, calls Quiyoughcohanock, on the south shore [of James River], or Salisbury side "— was probably the residence of this chief — *Strachey*, p 56 "Popham side" was on the north shore — See *Archæol. Amer*, vol iv pp. 42, 57

dent had sene him diûse tymes before. His conntynance was nothing cherefull, for we had not seen him since he was in the feild against vs: but the President would take no knowledge thereof, and vsed him kindely; giving him a red wascoat, wch he did desire.

Tapahanah did enquire after our shipping. He receyued answer as before. He said his ould store was spent; that his new was not at full growth by a foote; that, as soone as any was ripe, he would bring it, wch promise he truly pformed.

The . . [7] of . . . [7] Mr Kendall was put of from being of the Counsell, and comitted to prison; for that it did manyfestly appeare he did practize to sowe discord betweene the President and Councell.[8]

Sicknes had not now left us vj able men in our towne. God's onely mercy did now watch and warde for us but the President hidd this our weaknes carefully from the salvages, neuer suffring them, in all his tyme, to come into our towne.[9]

---

[7] Blanks in the original manuscript

[8] The first Council for the Colony, appointed in England, consisted of Edward Maria Wingfield, Bartholomew Gosnold, Christopher Newport, John Smith, John Ratcliffe, John Martin, George Kendall — *Smith's Virginia*, Appendix, p 3. Owing to suspicions entertained of Smith, he was not sworn of the Council till June 10, — twelve days before the return of Newport for England — *Ibid*, pp 5, 6, *Archæol Amer*, vol iv p 57 Kendall was deposed, probably, soon after the death of Gosnold — See *True Relation*, and *Percy* as above.

[9] Percy, one of the party, gives a sad picture of the sufferings endured by the colonists at this period How striking a parallel is presented to the condition of the Pilgrims at Plymouth during the first winter and spring! He gives a list of the names of nineteen persons who died in August, and five who died in September. "Our men," he says, ' were destroyed with cruel diseases — as swellings, fluxes, burning

Septem — The vjth of September, Pasyaheigh sent vs a boy that was run from vs. This was the first assurance of his peace wth vs; besides, wee found them no canyballs.[1]

The boye obserued the men & women to spend the most p^t of the night in singing or howling, and that euery morning the women carryed all the litle children to the river's sides; but what they did there, he did not knowe.

The rest of the wyroaunces doe likewise send our men runnagats to vs home againe, vsing them well during their being with them; so as now, they being well rewarded at home at their retorne, they take litle ioye to trauell abroad w^hout pasports.

---

fevers — and by wars, and some departed suddenly, but, for the most part, they died of mere famine. There were never Englishmen left in a foreign country in such misery as we were in this new-discovered Virginia. We watched every three nights, lying on the bare, cold ground, what weather soever came, warded all the next day, which brought our men to be most feeble wretches. Our food was but a small can of barley, sod in water, to fiue men a day, our drinke, cold water taken out of the river, which was at a flood very salt, at a low tide full of slime and filth, which was the destruction of many of our men. Thus we lived, for the space of five months, in this miserable distress, not having five able men to man our bulwarks upon any occasion. If it had not pleased God to have put a terrour in the Savages' hearts, we had all perished by those wild and cruel Pagans, being in that weak state as we were, our men night and day groaning in every corner of the fort, most pitiful to hear. If there were any conscience in men, it would make their hearts to bleed to hear the pitiful murmurings and outcries of our sick men, without relief, every night and day, for the space of six weeks, some departing out of the world, many times three or four in a night, in the morning, their bodies trailed out of their cabins, like dogs, to be buried. In this sort did I see the mortality of divers of our people" — *Purchas*, vol. iv. p 1690. " The living were scarce able to bury the dead" — " As yet, we had no houses to cover us; our tents were rotten, and our cabins worse than nought. The President and Capt. Martin's sickness constrained me to be Cape Marchant, and yet to spare no pains in making houses for the company" — *Smith's True Relation*.

[1] Smith believed that some of the Indians in the neighborhood of Jamestown were cannibals, and he gives a strange relation in proof of it, in connection with an account of their yearly sacrifices — *Smith's Virginia*, pp. 32, 33.

The Councell demanded some larger allowance for themselues, and for some sick, their fauorites; wch the President would not yeeld vnto, w^thout their warrants.

This matter was before ppounded by Captn. Martyn,² but so nakedly as that he neyther knew the quantity of the stoare to be but for xiij weekes and a half, under the Cap Merchaunt's³ hand. He prayed them further to consider the long tyme before wee expected Captn. Newport's retorne; the incertainty of his retorne, if God did not fauo^r his voyage; the long tyme before our haruest would bee ripe; and the doubtfull peace that wee had wth the Indyans, wch they would keepe no longer then oportunity served to doe vs mischeif.

It was then therefore ordered that euery meale of fish or fleshe should excuse the allowance for poridg, both against the sick and hole. The Councell, therefore, sitting againe upon this proposition, instructed in the former reasons and order, did not thinke fit to break the former order by enlarging their allowance, as will appeare by the most voyces reddy to be shewed vnder their handes. Now was the comon store of oyle, vinigar, sack, & aquavite all spent, saueing twoe gallons of each. the sack reserued for the Comunion Table, the rest for such extreamityes as might fall upon us, w^ch

---

² Martin was one of the original Colonial Council — *Ante*, p 17, note 8.

³ His majesty's orders for the government of the Colonies provided for the appointment of one person in each Colony to be " Treasurer, or Cape-merchant, of the same "— *Stith*, p. 39. Thomas Studley was the first who filled that office in Virginia Among the deaths this year in August, recorded by Percy, in Purchas, as above, is that of " Thomas Stoodie, Cape-merchant " This would seem to be no other than Studley, yet his name appears, in the Appendix to Smith's Virginia, as a narrator of events which took place after the above date. It is quite likely that the editor of these narratives misapprehended, in some particulars, as to their authorship

the President had onely made knowne to Captn. Gosnold; of wch course he liked well. The vessells wear, therefore, boonged vpp. When Mr Gosnold was dead, the President did acquaint the rest of the Counsell wth the said remnant: but, Lord, how they then longed for to supp up that little remnant! for they had nowe emptied all their own bottles, and all other that they could smell out.

A little while after this, the Councell did againe fall vpon the President for some better allowance for themselves, and some few the sick, their privates. The President ptested he would not be partial; but, if one had any thing of him, euery man should have his portion according to their placs. Neuertheless, that, vpon their warrants, he would deliuer what pleased them to demand. Yf the President had at that tyme enlarged the pportion according to their request, w̃hout doubt, in very short tyme, he had starued the whole company. He would not ioyne wth them, therefore, in such ignorant murder w̃hout their own warrant.

The President, well seeing to what end their ympacience would growe, desired them earnestly & often tymes to bestow the Presidentshipp amonge themselues; that he would obey, a private man, as well as they could comand. But they refused to dischaige him of the place; sayeing they monght not doe it, for that hee did his Matie good service in yt. In this meane tyme, the Indians did daily relieue us wth corne and fleshe, that, in three weekes, the President had reared vpp xx men able to worke; for, as his stoare increased, he mended the comon pott he had laid vp, besides, prouision for 3 weekes' wheate before hand.

By this tyme, the Councell had fully plotted to depose Wingfield, ther then President, and had drawne certeyne artycles in wrighting amongst themselues, and toke their oathes vpon the Evangelists to obserue them: th' effect whereof was, first,—

To depose the then President;

To make Mr Ratcliffe[4] the next President,

Not to depose the one th' other,

Not to take the deposed President into Councell againe,

Not to take Mr Archer into the Councell, or any other, wthout the consent of euery one of them. To theis they had subscribed; as out of their owne mouthes, at seuerall tymes, it was easily gathered. Thus had they forsaken his Ma^{ts} governm^t, sett vs downe in the instrucc͠ons, & made it a Triumvirat.

It seemeth Mr Archer was nothing acquainted wth theis artycles. Though all the rest crept out of his noats and comentaryes that were preferred against the President, yet it pleased God to cast him into the same disgrace and pitt that he prepared for another, as will appeare hereafter.

Septem. — The 10 of September, Mr Ratcliff, Mr Smyth,[5] and Mr Martynn, came to the President's tennt with a warrant,

---

[4] John Ratcliffe was captain of the pinnace on the voyage from England, and one of the original Colonial Council.—See *Smith's Virginia*, Appendix, p 3, *ante*, p 17, note 8. He gave great dissatisfaction as President, which office he held one year, and was succeeded by Smith. He went to England soon after, but in May or June, 1609, set sail for Virginia as captain of one of the ships which accompanied Somers and Gates. He, with thirty or forty others, was slain by Powhatan in 1610.—See *Smith's Virginia*, Appendix, pp 93, 105. *Strachey*, in Purchas, vol iv p. 1734.

[5] Capt John Smith, so famous in Virginia and New-England history.

subscribed vnder their handes, to depose the President; sayeing they thought him very unworthy to be eyther P*sident or of the Councell, and therefore discharged him of bothe. He answered them, that they had eased him of a great deale of care and trouble; that, long since, hee had diuers tymes profered them the place at an easier rate; and, further, that the President ought to be remoued (as appeareth in his Ma⁺ˢ instrucc̃õns for our government) by the greater number of xiij voyces, Councellors,[6] that they were but three,[7] and therefore wished them to proceede advisedly. But they told him, if they did him wrong, they must answere it. Then said the deposed President, "I ame at your pleasure: dispose of me as you will, wᵗʰout further garboiles."

I will now write what followeth in my owne name, and giue the new President his title. I shall be the briefer being thus discharged. I was comytted to a Serieant, and sent to the pynnasse, but I was answered wᵗʰ, "If they did me wronge, they must answere it."

The 11ᵗʰ of September, I was sent for to come before the President and Councell vpon their Court daie. They had now made Mʳ Archer, Recorder of Virginia. The President made a speeche to the Collony, that he thought it fitt to

---

[6] The Charter of Virginia provided for a Colonial Council of thirteen, and his Majesty's instructions and orders authorized the major part of said Council, upon any just cause, to remove the President or any other of the Council. — *Stith*, p 37, and Appendix, p 8. There seems to have been a departure from this rule, at the first, in the appointment of only *seven* councillors.

[7] Newport had sailed for England, Gosnold had died, Kendall had been deposed, and, setting aside Wingfield, there remained of the Council only the above-named three.

acquaint them whie I was deposed. I ame now forced to stuff my paper with frivolous trifles, that our graue and worthy Councell may the better strike those vaynes where the corrupt blood lyeth, and that they may see in what manner of governm[t] the hope of the Collony now travayleth

Ffirst, Master President said that I had denyed him a penny whitle,[8] a chickyn, a spoonfull of beere, and serued him wth foule corne; and wth that pulled some graine out of a bagg, shewing it to the company.

Then start up M[r] Smyth, and said that I had told him playnly how he lied; and that I said, though we were equall heere, yet, if he were in England, he[9] would think scorne his man[1] should be my companyon.

M[r] Martyn followed w[th], "He reporteth that I doe slack the service in the Collonye, and doe nothing but tend my pott, spitt, and oven; but he hath starued my sonne, and denyed him a spoonefull of beere. I haue freinds in England shal be revenged on him, if euer he come in London"

I asked M[r] President if I should answere theis compl[ts], and whether he had ought els to charge me w[th]all. W[th] that he pulled out a paper booke, loaded full w[th] artycles against me, and gaue them M[r] Archer to reade.

I tould M[r] President and the Councell, that, by the instruccōns for our governm[t], our proceedings ought to be verball,[2]

---

[8] "Whittle," a small pocket-knife.

[9] Probably it should read "*I* would think scorn," &c.

[1] *Name?* See p 41, lines 27 and 28

[2] "These judicial proceedings should be made summarily and verbally, till they come to the judgment, or sentence, which should be briefly registered in a book kept for that purpose," &c — See the king s instructions and orders in *Stith*, pp 37-41

and I was there ready to answere; but they said they would proceede in that order. I desired a coppie of the articles, and tyme giuen me to answere them likewise by wrighting; but that would not be graunted. I badd them then please themselues. Mr Archer then read some of the artycles, when, on the suddaine, Mr President said, "Staie, staie! Wee know not whether he will abide our Judgment, or whether he will appeale to the King;" sayeing to me, "How saie you? Will you appeale to the King, or no?" I apprehended presently that God's mercy had opened me a waie, through their ignorance, to escape their malice; for I never knew how I might demande an appeale besides, I had secret knowledge how they had foreiudged me to paie fiue fold for any thing that came to my handes, whereof I could not discharge myself by wrighting, and that I should lie in prison vntil I had paid it.

The Cape Marchant had deliured me our marchandize, w^thout any noat of the perticularyties, vnder my hand; for himself had receyued them in grosse. I likewise, as occation moued me, spent them in trade or by guift amongst the Indians. So likewise did Captn. Newport take of them, when he went up to discouer the King's river, what he thought good, w^thout any noate of his hand mentioning the certainty; and disposed of them as was fitt for him. Of these, likewise, I could make no accompt; onely I was well assured I had neuer bestowed the valewe of three penny whitles to my own vse, nor to the private vse of any other; for I never carryed any fauorite over wth me, or intertayned any thear. I was all one and one to all.

Vpon theis consideracōns, I answered Mr President and the Councell, that His Mat^{ys} handes were full of mercy, and that I did appeale to His Ma^{ts} mercy. They then comytted me prisoner againe to the master of ye pynnasse, wth theis words, "Looke to him well. he is now the King's prisoner."

Then Mr Archer pulled out of his bosome another paper book full of artycles against me, desiring that he might reade them in the name of the Collony. I said I stood there ready to answere any man's complaintt whome I had wronged; but no one man spoke one word against me. Then was he willed to reade his booke, whereof I complayned; but I was still answered, "If they doe me wrong, they must answer it." I have forgotten the most of the artycles, they were so slight (yet he glorieth much in his pennworke). I know well the last· and a speeche that he then made savoured well of a mutyny; for he desired that by no means I might lye prysoner in the towne, least boath he and others of the Collony should not giue such obedience to their comaund as they ought to doe: which goodly speech of his they easilye swallowed.

But it was vsuall and naturall to this honest gent., Mr Archer, to be allwayes hatching of some mutany in my tyme. Hee might haue appeared an author of 3 seuerall mutynies.

And hee (as Mr Pearsie[8] sent me worde) had bought some

---

[8] "This was the Honorable Mr. George Percy, of the ancient family of the Percys so renowned in story, and brother to the Earl of Northumberland Neither did his actions here disgrace the nobility of his birth, for he justly obtained the reputation of a gentleman of great honor, courage, and industry He seems to have come merely a volunteer upon the expedition, and bore no post or office of government " — *Stith*, p 45 Percy subsequently became temporary Governor of the Colony, of which he wrote an interesting account from its commencement The early portion was printed by Purchas, and is referred to above

witnesses' handes against me to diuers artycles, wth Indian cakes (wch was noe great matter to doe after my deposal, and considering their hungar), perswations, and threats. At another tyme, he feared not to saie openly, and in the presence of one of the Councell, that, if they had not deposed me when they did, he hadd gotten twenty others to himself wch should haue deposed me. But this speech of his was likewise easily disiested.[4] Mr Crofts[5] feared not to saie, that, if others would ioyne wth him, he would pull me out of my seate, and out of my skynn too. Others would saie (whose names I spare), that, vnless I would amend their allowance, they would be their owne caruers. For these mutinus speeches I rebuked them openly, and proceeded no further against them, considering thein of men's liues in the King's service there. One of the Councell was very earnest wth me to take a guard aboute me. I answered him, I would no guard but God's love and my own innocencie. In all theis disorders was Mr Archer a ringleader.

When Mr President and Mr Archer had made an end of their artycles aboue mentioned, I was again sent prisoner to the pynnasse; and Mr Kendall, takeinge from thence, had his liberty, but might not carry armes.

All this while, the salvages brought to the towne such corn and fflesh as they could spare. Paspaheighe, by Tapahanne's mediation, was taken into freindshipp with vs. The

---

[4] That is, *disiested*. *Disgest* was a very common form, in early writers, of the word we spell *digest*. — See Halliwell's "Archaic and Provincial Words."

[5] Richard Crofts, who is classed among the "gentlemen" in the list of the first planters. — *Smith's Virginia*, Appendix, p. 7.

Councillors, Mr Smyth especially, traded vp and downe the river wth the Indyans for corne; wch releued the Collony well.⁶

As I understand by a report, I am much charged wth staruing the Collony. I did alwaies giue enry man his allowance faithfully, both of corne, oyle, aquivite, &c, as was by the Counsell proportioned · neyther was it bettered after my tyme, untill, towards th' end of March, a bisket was allowed to euery workeing man for his breakfast, by means of the puision brought vs by Captn. Newport; as will appeare hereafter. It is further said, I did much banquit and ryot. I never had but one squirell roasted; whereof I gave part to Mr Ratcliff, then sick: yet was that squirell given me. I did never heate a flesh pott but when the comon pot was so used likewise. Yet how often Mr President's and the Councellors' spitts haue night & daye bene endaungered to break their backes,—so laden wth swanns, geese, ducks, &^c ! how many times their flesh potts haue swelled, many hungry eies did behold, to their great longing; and what great theeues and theeving thear hath been in the comon stoare since my tyme, I doubt not but is already made knowne to his Ma^ts Councell for Virginia.

The 17th daie of Septemb^r, I was sent for to the Court to answere a complaint exhibited against me by Jehu Robinson,⁷ for that, when I was President, I did saie, hee wth others had

---

⁶ Smith appears to have been indefatigable in his efforts to serve the Colony at this time An account of his various trading expeditions in search of corn will be found in the early tracts above cited

⁷ John Robinson is classed among the "gentlemen," in the list just referred to.

consented to run awaye with the shallop to Newfoundland. At an other tyme, I must answere Mr Smyth for that I had said hee did conceal an intended mutany. I tould Mr Recorder, those words would beare no actions, that one of the causes was done wthout the lymits menc̄ōned in the Patent graunted to vs; and therefore prayed Mr President that I mought not be thus lugged with theis disgraces and troubles but hee did weare no other eies or eares than grew on Mr Archer's head.

The jury gaue the one of them 100^h and the other two hundred pound damages for slaunder. Then Mr Recorder did very learnedly comfort me, that, if I had wrong, I might bring my writ of erior in London, whereat I smiled.

I, seeing their law so speedie and cheape, desired justice for a copper kettle wch Mr Crofte did deteyne from me Hee said I had giuen it him I did bid him bring his proofe for that Hee confessed he had no proofe. Then Mr President did aske me if I would be sworne I did not giue it him. I said I knew no cause whie to sweare for myne owne. He asked Mr Crofts if hee would make oath I did give it him; wch oathe he tooke, and wonn my kettle from me, that was in that place and tyme worth half his weight in gold. Yet I did understand afterwards that he would haue given John Capper the one half of the kettle to haue taken the oath for him; but hee would no copper on that price.

I tould Mr President I had not known the like lawe, and prayed they would be more sparing of law vntill wee had more witt or wealthe; that lawes were good spies in a populous, peaceable, and plentifull country, whear they did make the good men better, & stayed the badd from being worse; y^t wee weare so poore as they did but rob us of tyme that might be better ymployed in service in the Collonye.

The [7] . . . daie of [7] . . . the President did beat James Read, the Smyth.[8] The Smythe stroake him againe. For this he was condempned to be hanged; but, before he was turned of the lather, he desired to speak with the President in private, to whome he accused Mr Kendall of a mutiny, and so escaped himself [9] What indictment Mr Recorder framed against the Smyth, I knowe not; but I knowe it is familiar for the President, Counsellors, and other officers, to beate men at their pleasures. One lyeth sick till death, another walketh lame, the third cryeth out of all his boanes, wch myseryes they doe take vpon their consciences to come to them by this their almes of beating Wear this whipping, lawing, beating, and hanging, in Virginia, knowne in England, I fear it would driue many well affected myndes from this hono^{ble} action of Virginia.

This Smyth comyng aboord the pynnasse wth some others, aboute some busines, 2 or 3 dayes before his arraignem^t, brought me comendacõns from Mr Pearsye, Mr Waller,[1] Mr Kendall, and some others, saieing they would be glad to see

---

[7] Blanks in the original manuscript

[8] "James Read, Blacksmith" — *Smith's Virginia*, Appendix, p 8

[9] This account corresponds substantially with Smith in his True Relation, who says Kendall was tried by a jury Studley, in Smith's Virginia (Appendix, p 12), says that Kendall's crime had connection with a plot, formed in Smith's absence, to divert the course of the pinnace (which had been fitted up for a trading voyage), and "to go for England."

[1] "John Waler" is in the list of "gentlemen" — *Ibid*, p 7

me on shoare I answered him, they were honest gent., and had carryed themselues very obediently to their goūnors. I prayed God that they did not think of any ill thing vnworthie themselues. I added further, that vpon Sundaie, if the weathiar were faire, I would be at the sermon Lastly, I said that I was so sickly, starued, lame, and did lye so could and wett in the pynnasse, as I would be dragged thithere before I would goe thither any more. Sundaie proued not faire I went not to the sermon.

The [2] . . . daie of [2] . . ., Mr Kendall was executed; being shott to death for a mutiny. In th' arrest of his judgm^t, he alleaged to Mr President y^t his name was Sicklemore, not Ratcliff,[3] & so had no authority to pnounce judgm^t. Then Mr Martyn pnounced judgm^t.

Somewhat before this tyme, the President and Councell had sent for the keyes of my coffers, supposing that I had some wrightings concerning the Collony I requested that the Clearke of the Councell might see what they tooke out of my coffers; but they would not suffer him or any other. Vnder cullor heereof, they took my books of accompt, and all my noates that concerned the expences of the Collony, and instructions vnder the Cape-Marchant's hande of the stoare of prouision, diuers other bookes & trifles of my owne proper goods, wch I could neuer recover Thus was I made good prize on all sides.

---

[2] Blanks in the original manuscript.
[3] "Ratcliffe, whose right name was Sickelmore"—*Smith's Virginia*, Appendix, p 93 His name appears in the second charter of Virginia as "Capt. John Sicklemore, alias Ratcliffe"—*Stith*, Appendix, p 11

The[4] ... daie of[4] ..., the President comanded me to come on shore; wch I refused, as not rightfully deposed, and desired that I mought speake to him and the Councell in the p^rsence of 10 of the best sorte of the gent. W^th much intreaty, some of them wear sent for. Then I tould them I was determined to goe into England to acquaint our Councell there wth our weaknes. I said further, their lawes and governm^t was such as I had no ioye to liue under them any longer; that I did much myslike their triumverat haueing forsaken his Ma^ts instruccõns for our government, and therefore praied there might be more made of the Councell. I said further, I desired not to go into England, if eyther Mr President or Mr Archer would goe, but was willing to take my fortune wth the Collony; and did also proffer to furnish them wth 100^li towards the fetching home the Collonye, if the action was giuen ouer They did like of none of my proffers, but made diuers shott att mee in the pynnasse I, seeing their resoluc̃ons, went ashoare to them, wheare, after I had staied a while in conference, they sent me to the pynnasse againe.

Decem.—The 10th of December, Mr Smyth went vp the ryuer of the Chechohomynies[5] to trade for corne. He was desirous to see the heade of that riuer; and, when it was not passible wth the shallop, he hired a cannow and an Indian to carry him vp further. The riuer the higher grew worse and worse. Then hee went on shoare wth his guide, and left

---

[4] Blanks in the original manuscript.
[5] This riuer empties into the James River on the north side, a few miles above Jamestown.

Robinson & Emmery,[6] twoe of our Men, in the cannow, wch were presently slayne by the Indians, Pamaonke's men, and hee himself taken prysoner, and, by the means of his guide, his lief was saved; and Pamaonché, haueing him prisoner, carryed him to his neybors wyroances to see if any of them knew him for one of those wch had bene, some twoe or three yeeres before vs, in a river amongst them Northward, and taken awaie some Indians from them by force. At last he brought him to the great Powaton (of whome before wee had no knowledg),[7] who sent him home to our towne the viij^th of January[8]

---

[6] John Robinson is in the list of "gentlemen," and "Tho Emry" is in the list of "carpenters"—See *Smith*, as above

[7] See p 15

[8] It was while on this expedition, as we are told in one of the later publications of Smith, that his life, which was threatened by Powhatan, was saved by his daughter Pocahontas, just as he was about to suffer The story is an interesting and romantic one But the critical reader of the accounts of Smith's adventures in Virginia will be struck with the fact, that no mention whatever is made of this incident in his minute personal narrative covering this period, written at the time, on the spot, and published in 1608, nor in the narrative of his companions, in the appendix to the tract of 1612, in neither of which is any attempt made to conceal his valiant exploits and hair-breadth escapes. In his "New England's Trials" (1622) is a brief incidental allusion, in an ambiguous form, to his having been "delivered" by Pocahontas, when taken prisoner But the current story first appears in the "Generall Historie," first published in 1624 This book is compiled chiefly from earlier publications of his own and others, and what relates to Virginia, for this early period, is taken for the most part from the tract of 1612, though there is an occasional variation in the text, and incidents related in the tract of 1608 are sometimes introduced In the tract last named, written by Smith himself on the spot, it does not appear that he considered his life at all in danger while he was a guest or prisoner of Powhatan The hazards which he had run when he was first surprised by the Indians, and while in the hands of the King of Pamaunkey—who took him prisoner after the slaughter of his only two companions—and of the other minor chiefs, were ended. The whole bearing of the emperor towards him from the first, far from being hostile or even unfriendly, was in every respect kind and hospitable. The emperor, says Smith, "kindly received me

During Mr Smythe's absence, the President did swear Mr Archer one of the Councell, contrary to his oath taken in the artycles agreed vpon betweene themselues (before spoken

---

with good words, and great platters of sundry victuals, assuring me of his friendship, and my liberty in four days." A conversation then ensued between them, which evidently resulted in inspiring mutual confidence. The savage was curious to know what brought Smith into the country, and appeared satisfied with the answers he received, which were far from the truth. He informed Smith as to the extent of his dominions, the character of the neighboring tribes, &c., and his guest "requited his discourse" by "describing to him the territories of Europe which were subject to our great king, . . the innumerable multitude of ships, the terrible manner of fighting" under Capt. Newport, whose "greatness he admired, and not a little feared. He desired me to forsake Paspahegh, and to live with him upon his river. And thus having, with all the kindness he could devise, sought to content me, he sent me home with four men,— one that usually carried my gown and knapsack after me, two others loaded with bread, and one to accompany me." This simple story of Smith's interview with Powhatan,— here considerably abridged,— in which the name of the Indian child Pocahontas is not even mentioned, shows quite a different treatment from what is indicated in the following passage, subsequently interpolated in the most abrupt and awkward manner into the account in the "Generall Historie." After describing the stately appearance of Powhatan in the midst of his courtiers and women, somewhat as in the former account, the latter narrative proceeds to say, that, on Smith's entrance before the king, the people gave a great shout. The Queen of Appamatuck was deputed to bring him water to wash his hands, and another brought him a bunch of feathers, instead of a towel, to dry them. Then, "having feasted him after the best barbarous manner they could, a long consultation was held, but the conclusion was, two great stones were brought before Powhatan. Then as many as could laid hands on him, dragged him to them, and thereon laid his head, and, being ready with their clubs to beat out his brains, Pocahontas, the king's dearest daughter, when no entreaty could prevail, got her head in his arms, and laid her own upon his, to save him from death; whereat the emperor was contented he should live to make him hatchets, and her, bells, beads," &c. After some days, the emperor came to him, and told him they now were friends, and presently he should go to Jamestown, where, with twelve guides, he soon sent him.

No one can doubt that the earlier narrative contains the truer statement, and that the passage last cited is one of the few or many embellishments with which Smith, with his strong love of the marvellous, was disposed to garnish the stories of his early adventures, and with which he or his editors were tempted to adorn particularly his later works. The name of Pocahontas, afterwards the "Lady Rebecca," had become

of), and contrary to the King's instrucc͠ons, and w^thout Mr Martyn's consent; whereas there weare no more but the President and Mr Martyn then of the Councell.

---

somewhat famous in the annals of Virginia, since the time Smith knew her there at the age of thirteen or fourteen, when he left the Colony for England. From her position, she had been the means of rendering the Colony some service. Through her, an influence for good had been acquired over Powhatan. As the daughter of an emperor,—possessing, as is said, some personal attractions, and the first convert of her tribe to Christianity,—she had been, on her visit to England with her husband, John Rolfe, in 1616, an object of much curiosity and attention. The temptation, therefore, to bring her on the stage as a heroine in a new character in connection with Smith, always the hero of his chronicles,—and who, in his early adventures in the East, as he subsequently claimed, had inspired the gentle Tragabigzanda with the tenderest emotions towards him,—appears to have been too great for him to withstand, and was not to be resisted by those interested in getting up the "Generall Historie," and therefore, in reproducing the account of his imprisonment, this story — the substance of which Smith appears to have intimated to her majesty Queen Anne, in general terms, while the "Lady Rebecca" was in England ("Generall Historie," p. 121) — is introduced for the first time into the narrative of this portion of his adventures.

It should be borne in mind, that Smith makes no claim to have been taken prisoner more than once by the Indians, during his residence of two years and a half in Virginia. All his adventures during this period are related in detail, and there was but one occasion on which the service claimed to have been rendered by Pocahontas could have been performed. This marvellous story finds no proper place in any other adventure, and the introduction of it into the narrative in the "Generall Historie" is equivalent to setting aside the whole of the earlier account, so far as relates to the manner of his reception and his whole treatment by Powhatan, when brought before him a prisoner.

In its connection with this subject, the passage in the text of Wingfield, at this place, becomes especially significant, as giving the main features of Smith's imprisonment as they were understood at Jamestown at the time, and, of course, as told by Smith himself. According to this, as we have seen, his life was imperilled only at the time of his first falling into the hands of the Indians,—"Pamaunkey's men," and he was saved by his Indian guide. The passage is silent as to Pocahontas, and the name of Powhatan is introduced only in connection with the fact, that, when Smith was brought before him a prisoner, he sent the captive home to Jamestown.

To those familiar with Secretary Hamor's rare tract on Virginia, published in 1615, which is largely devoted to Pocahontas, his silence will be deemed equally significant.

Mr Archer, being settled in his authority, sought how to call Mr Smyth's lief in question, and had indited him vpon a chapter in Leuiticus for the death of his twoe men.[9] He had had his tryall the same daie of his retorne, and, I believe, his hanging the same or the next daie, so speedie is our lawe there. But it pleased God to send Captn. Newport vnto us the same evening, to o^r vnspeakable comfort, whose arrivall saued Mr Smyth's leif and mine, because hee took me out of the pynnasse, and gaue me leave to lye in the towne. Also by his comyng was p^{r}vented a parliam^t,[1] wch ye newe Counsailo^r, Mr Recorder, intended thear to summon. Thus error begot error.

Captayne Newport, haueing landed, lodged, and refreshed his men, ymploied some of them about a faire stoare

---

Without designing to impeach the general trustworthiness of Smith's original narrations, and with no disposition to detract from the "Generall Historie" (a large part of which is compiled from writings of others) and the "True Travels," to the extent implied in Burk's designation of the former as an "epic history or romance" (see Burk's History of Virginia, preface), it must be admitted that the tendency to exaggeration and over-statement in these later publications is evident. Referring to what has already been said, it would be curious to trace other variations in the two accounts of Smith's imprisonment especially referred to, — in the "True Relation" and in the "Generall Historie." But this note is already too much extended. An admirable analysis of Smith's "Generall History" and "True Travels" may be found in Palfrey's History of New England, vol. i. pp. 89–93.

[9] "Some, no better than they should be, had plotted with the President, the next day, to have put him to death by the Levitical law, for the lives of Robinson and Emry, pretending the fault was his," &c. — *Smith's Generall Historie*, p. 49. Smith, probably, was to be tried by the spirit of the law laid down in Lev. xxiv. 19–21.

[1] If, by a parliament, is here intended the whole body of colonists or their representatives, it is certain that no authority for summoning such an assembly was vested in the Council or Colony — *Stith*, pp. 37–41.

house, others about a stove, and his maryners aboute a church;² all wch workes they finished cherefully and in short tyme.

January. — The 7 of January,³ our towne was almost quite

---

² The narrative, in the Appendix to Smith, complains that the mariners spent much time hunting for gold, kept the ship long in the country (fourteen weeks), consuming their food, "that the mariners might say they built such a golden church, that we can say the rain washed to near nothing in fourteen days."

Smith thus describes "what churches we had, order of service," &c., when he first went to Virginia. "When I went first to Virginia, I well remember, we did hang an awning (which is an old sail) to three or four trees to shadow us from the sun. Our walls were rails of wood, our seats, unhewed trees, till we cut planks, our pulpit, a bar of wood nailed to two neighbouring trees. In foul weather, we shifted into an old rotten tent, for we had few better, and this came by the way of adventure for new. This was our church, till we built a homely thing like a barn, set upon cratchets, covered with rafts, sedge, and earth, so was also the walls. the best of our houses of the like curiosity, but the most part far much worse workmanship, that could neither well defend wind nor rain. Yet we had daily Common Prayer morning and evening, every Sunday two sermons, and every three months the holy Communion, till our minister [Mr. Hunt, the date of whose death is uncertain] died, but our Prayers daily, with an Homily on Sundays, we continued two or three years after, till more preachers came. And surely God did most mercifully hear us, till the continual inundations of mistaking directions, factions, and numbers of unprovided Libertines, near consumed us all, as the Israelites in the wilderness." — *Smith's* "Advertisements," &c., London, 1631, pp. 32, 33.

³ According to the dates in the text, this fire took place the day before the arrival of Newport, but Smith says, "Within five or six days after the arrival of the ship, by a mischance our Fort was burned, and the most of our apparel, lodging, and private provision. Many of our old men diseased, and [many] of our new, for want of lodging, perished." — *True Relation.* The inference from the account in the Appendix to Smith's Virginia is clear, that Newport had arrived some time before the fire took place. If the ship remained at Jamestown "fourteen weeks," as is stated in the tract last named, — sailing for England, April 10, — it would show that she arrived some days earlier than the date given in the text. Smith and Wingfield agree as to the arrival of Newport on the evening of the day of the former's return from his captivity among the Indians.

burnt,[4] with all our apparell and prouision;[5] but Captn Newport healed our wants, to our great comforts, out of the great plenty sent vs by the prouident and loving care of our worthie and most worthie Councell.

This vigilant Captayne, slacking no oportunity that might advaunce the prosperity of the Collony, haueing setled the company vppon the former workes, took Mr Smyth and Mr Scrivenor[6] (another Councellor of Virginia, vpon whose discretion liveth a great hope of the action), went to discouer the River Pamaonche, on the further side whearof dwelleth the Great Powaton, and to trade wth him for corne. This River lieth North from vs, and runneth East and West. I haue

---

[4] "The houses first raised were all burnt, by a casualty of fire, the beginning of the second year of their seat, and in the second voyage of Capt. Newport, which since have been better rebuilded, though as yet in no great uniformity either for the fashion or beauty of the street. A delicate-wrought, fine kind of mat the Indians make, with which (as they can be trucked for or snatched up) our people do dress their chambers and inward roomes, which make their houses so much the more handsome. The houses have wide and large country chimneys, in the which is to be supposed (in such plenty of wood) what fires are maintained and they have found the way to cover their houses now (as the Indians) with the barks of trees, as durable, and as good proof against storms and winter weather, as the best tyle, defending likewise the piercing sunbeams of summer, and keeping the inner lodgings cool enough, which before, in sultry weather, would be like stoves, whilst they were, as at first, pargetted and plastered with bitumen or tough clay. And, thus armed for the injury of changing times and seasons of the year, we hold ourselves well apaid, though wanting arras hangings, tapestry, and gilded Venetian cordovan, or more spruce household garniture and wanton city ornaments "—*Strachey*, in Purchas, vol iv p 1753

[5] "Good Mr Hunt, our preacher, lost all his library, and all that he had but the clothes on his back; yet none ever saw him repine. This happened in the winter of that extreme frost, 1607"—*Smith's Virginia*, Appendix, p 20

[6] Matthew Scrivener, one of the second supply with Newport. He, with ten others, was drowned in a skiff, within a year from this time—*Ibid*, p 71.

nothing but by relation of that matter, and therefore dare not make any discourse thereof, lest I mought wrong the great desart wch Captn. Newport s loue to the action hath deserued; espially himself being present, and best able to giue satisfaccōn thereof. I will hasten, therefore, to his retorne.

March.— The 9th of March, he retorned to James Towne wth his pynnasse well loaden wth corne, wheat, beanes, and pease, to our great comfort & his worthi comendacōns.[7]

By this tyme, the Counsell & Captayne, haueing intentiuely looked into the carryadge both of the Councellors and other officers, remoued some officers out of the stoare, and Captn. Archer, a Councellor whose insolency did looke vpon that litle himself wth great sighted spectacles, derrogating from others' merrits by spueing out his venemous libells and infamous chronicles vpon them, as doth appeare in his owne hand wrighting, ffor w^ch, and other worse tricks, he had not escaped ye halter, but that Captn Newport interposed his advice to the contrary.

Captayne Newport, haneing now dispatched all his busines[8] and set the clocke in a true course (if so the Councell will keep it), prepared himself for England vpon the xth of

---

[7] A minute account of this trading expedition, during which Capt Newport for the first time had an interview with the "great Powhatan," and from which the forty who embarked on it returned with two or three hundred bushels of corn, may be seen in the "True Relation," and a more brief account in the Appendix to Smith's Virginia

[8] Newport, being warmly seconded by Capt Mutin, though against the advice of Smith, loaded the ship home with "gilded dirt," supposing it to be gold-dust — *Ibid*, pp 21 22

Aprill,[9] and arryued at Blackwall on Sunday, the xxjth of Maye, 1608.

FINIS.

I humbly craue some patience to answere many scandalus imputacōns wch malice, more than malice, hath scattered vpon my name, and those fiivolous three names obiected against me by the President and Councell; and though nil conscire sibi be the onely maske that can well couer my blushes, yett doe I not doubt but this my appologie shall easily wipe them awaie

It is noised that I combyned wth the Spanniards to the distrucōn of the Collony, That I ame an atheist, because I carryed not a Bible wth me, and because I did forbid the preacher to preache; that I affected a kingdome, That I did hide of the comon prouision in the ground.

I confesse I haue alwayes admyred any noble vertue & prowesse, as well in the Spanniards (as in other nations), but naturally I haue alwayes distrusted and disliked their neighborhoode. I sorted many bookes in my house, to be sent vp to me at my goeing to Virginia; amongst them a Bible They were sent me vp in a trunk to London, wth diuers fruite, conserues, & p^{e}serues, wch I did sett in Mr Crofts his house in

---

[9] "He set sail for England the tenth of April Master Scrivener and myself, with our shallop, accompanied him to Cape Hendrick"—*True Relation* Wingfield, the author of this narrative, and Archer, returned home at this time with Capt Newport Archer came back to Virginia the next year, as master of one of the ships—in company with Gates and Somers—which left England in May or June, 1609—See *Smith's Virginia*, Appendix, pp 22, 93, *Strachey*, in Purchas, vol iv p 1734

Ratcliff[1] In my beeing at Virginia, I did vnderstand my trunk was thear broken vp, much lost, my sweetmeates eaten at his table, some of my bookes wch I missed to be seene in his hands; and whether amongst them my Bible was so ymbeasiled or mislayed by my seruants, and not sent me, I knowe not as yet.

Two or three Sundayes mornings, the Indians gave vs allarums at our towne By that tymes they weare answered, the place about us well discouered, and our devyne seivice ended, the daie was farr spent. The preacher did aske me if it were my pleasure to haue a sermon hee said hee was prepared for it I made answere, that our men were weary and hungry, and that he did see the time of the daie farr past (for at other tymes hee neuer made such question, but, the service finished, he began his sermon); & that, if it pleased him, wee would spare him till some other tyme. I never failed to take such noates by wrighting out of his doctrine as my capacity could comprehend, vnless some raynie day hindred my indeauo^r. My mynde never swelled with such ympossible mountebank humors as could make me affect any other kingdome then the kingdom of heaven

As truly as God hueth, I gave an ould man, then the keeper of the private stoure, 2 glasses wth sallet oyle wch I brought wth me out of England for my private stoare, and willed him to bury it in the ground, for that I feared the great heate

---

[1] Probably the hamlet of Ratcliffe, which is in the southern division of the parish of Stepney, about one mile from London — See *Lyson's Environs of London*, vol. ii. pp 712-15

would spoile it. Whatsoeuer was more, I did never consent vnto or knewe of it; and as truly was it protested vnto me, that all the remaynder before mencõned of the oyle, wyne, &c, wch the President receyued of me when I was deposed, they themselues poored into their owne bellyes.

To the President's and Councell's obiections I saie, that I doe knowe curtesey and civility became a governor. No penny whitle was asked me, but a kniffe, whereof I had none to spare. The Indyans had long before stoallen my knife. Of chickins I never did eat but one, and that in my sicknes. Mr Ratcliff had before that time tasted of 4 or 5. I had by my owne huswiferie bred aboue 37, and the most part of them of my owne poultrye; of all w^ch, at my comyng awaie, I did not see three hueing. I never denyed him (or any other) beare, when I had it. The corne was of the same wch wee all liued vpon.

Mr Smyth, in the tyme of our hungar, had spread a rumor in the Collony, that I did feast myself and my seruants out of the comon stoare, wth entent (as I gathered) to haue stirred the discontented company against me. I tould him privately, in Mr Gosnold's tent, that indeede I had caused half a pint of pease to be sodden wth a peese of pork, of my own prouision, for a poore old man, wch in a sicknes (whereof he died) he much desired; and said, that if out of his malice he had given it out otherwise, that hee did tell a leye. It was proued to his face that he begged in Ireland, like a rogue, w^thout a lycence. To such I would not my name should be a companyon.

Mr Martin's payns, during my comaund, never stirred out of

our towne tenn scoare; and how slack hee was in his watching and other dutyes, it is too well knowne. I never defrauded his sonne of any thing of his own allowance, but gaue him aboue it. I believe their disdainefull vsage and threats, which they many tymes gaue me, would have pulled some distempered speeches out of fare greater pacyence than myne. Yet shall not any revenging humor in me befoule my penn wth their base names and liues here and there. I did visit Mr Pearsie, Mr Hunt, Mr Brewster, Mr Pickasse, Mr Allicock, ould Short the bricklayer,[2] and diuerse others, at seuerall tymes. I never miskalled at a gent. at any tyme.

Concerning my deposing from my place, I can well proue that Mr Ratcliff said, if I had vsed him well in his sicknes (wherein I find not myself guilty of the contrary), I had never bene deposed.

Mr Smyth said, if it had not bene for Mr Archer, I hadd never bene deposed. Since his being here in the towne, he hath said that he tould the President and Councell that they were frivolous obiections they had collected against me, and that they had not done well to depose me. Yet, in my conscience, I doe believe him the first & onely practizer in theis practisses. Mr Archer's quarrell to me was, because hee had not the choice of the place for our plantation; because I mis-

---

[2] The name of "Mr. Robert Hunt, Preacher," is in the list of first planters — See pp 43, 44 "William Bruster, gentleman," died Aug 10, 1607, "of a wound given by the Savages, and was buried the eleventh day" "Dru Pickhouse" was one of the first planters "The nineteenth day [of August] died Drue Piggase, gentleman" "The fourteenth day [of August], Jerome Alikock, Ancient, died of a wound" — *Percy*, in Purchas, as above "Old Short's" name is not among the first planters The list is not complete.

liked his leying out of our towne, in the pinnasse; because I would not sware him of the Councell for Virginia, wch neyther I could doe or he deserve.

Mr Smyth's quarrell, because his name was mencõned in the entended & confessed mutiny by Galthropp³

Thomas Wootton, the surieon, because I would not subscribe to a warrant (wch he had gotten drawne) to the Treasurer of Virginia, to deliuer him money to furnish him wth druggs and other necessaryes, & because I disallowed his living in the pinnasse, haueing many of o^r men lyeing sick & wounded in o^r towne, to whose dressings by that meanes he slacked his attendance.

Of the same men, also, Captn Gosnold gaue me warning, misliking much their dispositions, and assured me they would lay hold of me if they could; and peradventure many, because I held them to watching, warding, and workeing; and the Collony generally, because I would not giue my consent to starue them. I cannot rack one word or thought from myself, touching my carryadg in Virginia, other than is herein set down.

If I may now, at the last, p^esume vpon yor favours, I am an hble suitor that your owne loue of truth will vouchsafe to releave me from all false aspertions happining since I embarked me into this affaire of Virginia. For my first worke (wch was to make a right choice of a spirituall pastor),⁴ I ap-

---

³ "Stephen Galthrope" died the fifteenth day of August, 1607.—*Percy*, as above

⁴ Mr Hunt, the preacher, is here referred to

"On the 19th of December, 1606, we set sail, but, by unprosperous winds, were kept six weeks in the sight of England all which time, Mr Hunt, our Preacher, was so weak and sick, that few expected his recovery. Yet, although he were but ten or

peale to the remembraunce of my Lo. of Caunt: his grace, who gaue me very gracious audience in my request. And the world knoweth whome I took wth me· truly, in my opinion, a man not any waie to be touched wth the rebellious humors of a popish spirit, nor blemished wth ye least suspition of a factius scismatick, whereof I had a spiall care. For other obiections, if yor worthie selues be pleased to set me free, I haue learned to despise ye populer verdict of ye vulgar. I ever chered up myself wth a confidence in ye wisdome of graue, iudicious senato^rs; & was never dismayed, in all my service, by any synister event though I bethought me of ye hard beginnings, w^ch, in former ages, betided those worthy spirits that planted the greatest monarchies in Asia & Europe, wherein I obserued rather ye troubles of Moses & Aron, with other of like history, then that venom in the mutinous brood of Cadmus, or that harmony in ye swete consent of Amphion. And when, wth ye former, I had considered that even the betheien, at their plantaĉon of the Romaine Empire, were not free from mortall hatred & intestine garboile, likewise

---

twelve miles from his habitation (the time we were in the Downs), and notwithstanding the stormy weather, noi the scandalous imputations (of some few little better than Atheists, of the greatest rank among us) suggested against him, all this could never force from him so much as a seeming desire to leave the business," &c — *Smith's Virginia*, Appendix, p 2

"It is evident [from the above] that Robert Hunt's habitation must have been in Kent, and I find, in Hasted's History of Kent (vol iii p 640), that Robert Hunt, A M, was appointed to the vicarage of Reculver, Jan 18, 1594; and that he resigned it in 1602. I cannot find, in the list of the Kentish Clergy at that time, any other Mr Hunt who bore the same Christian name, and, coupling the date of the resignation above stated with the period at which the first pastor of the English Colony must have been contemplating his departure to America, I think it most probable that he was the Vicar of Reculver "— *Anderson's History of the Church of England in the Colonies*, vol i pp 169, 170

that both yͤ Spanish & English records are guilty of like factions, it made me more vigilant in the avoyding thereof. and I ptest, my greatest contenc̄on was to pᵉvent contenc̄on, and my chiefest endeavour to p̃serue the liues of others, though wᵗʰ great hazard of my own; for I neuer desired to enamell my name wᵗʰ bloude. I reioice that my trauells & daungers haue done somewhat for the behoof of Jerusalem in Virginia. If it be obiected as my ouersight to put my self amongst such men, I can saie for myself, thear wear not any other for oʳ consort; & I could not forsake yᵉ enterprise of opening so glorious a kingdom vnto yᵉ King, wherein I shall ever be most ready to bestow yᵉ poore remainder of my dayes, as in any other his heighnes' dissignes, according to my bounden duty, wᵗʰ yᵘ vtmost of my poore tallent.[5]

---

[5] In the "Visitation of the County of Huntingdon, under the authority of William Camden," in 1613, I find an Edward Maria Wingfield (without doubt, our author) then living, unmarried, "of Stonley Prioɪye in comit. Hunt. jam superstes, 1613." He belonged to a distinguished family. His father was "Thomas Maria Wingfield, who was christened by Queene Mary and Cardinall Poole." His grandfather was "Sʳ Rich' Wingfeild of Kimbolton Castle, in Hunt, k, 12ᵗʰ sonne of Sʳ John Wingfeild of Letheringham, k, and of his wiffe Elizab Fitz-Lewis." Sɪʳ Richard "was Chancellor of the Duchie of Lanc, Lord-Deputy of Callis, and made K. of the Garter by Henɪ 8. His 1 wiffe was Katherine, Dutchess of Bedfrod and Buckingham, ..by whom Sʳ Rich' had no issue 2ᵈˡʸ, he maried Bridgett, da. and heire of Sʳ John Wilshire, and had all his children by her. He is buried at Toledo in Spayne."

When desired, books will be delivered to a reader at the desk indicated on the face of this ticket

Tickets for such books must be left at the delivery desk and delivery will be made when the immediate demand at the desk is satisfied

CORNELL UNIVERSITY LIBRARY

READING ROOM REGULATIONS.

1 The books on the shelves of this room are for free consultation and use in this room only Each volume, when done with, is to be returned to its place on the shelves

2 Readers must return all books drawn on this ticket to the delivery desk before leaving the room Every reader will be held responsible for works drawn in his name so long as his tickets remain unclaimed Returned tickets of works wanted again should be preserved, thereby avoiding the necessity of looking them out in the catalogue when again wanted.

3 Any reader having works in constant use can have them set aside for him by inserting a reserve book mark in each volume on its return to the desk Slips for this purpose can be obtained at the desk.

4 Books deposited in seminaries may be drawn at the desk for use in the reading room The regular demand for books from the stacks takes precedence over the request for books from seminary rooms.

5 The library does not undertake to provide language dictionaries for general use except such as are on the shelves of the reading room Students working in the seminary rooms will find the necessary lexicons there They must not be taken from these rooms for use elsewhere about the building.